Edible French

Tasty Expressions and Cultural Bites

CLOTILDE DUSOULIER

Illustrations by Mélina Josserand

A PERIGEE BOOK

For my parents,
who raised me in a
world of words.

A PERIGEE BOOK
Published by the Penguin Group
Penguin Group (USA) LLC
375 Hudson Street, New York, New York 10014

USA · Canada · UK · Ireland · Australia · New Zealand · India · South Africa · China

penguin.com

A Penguin Random House Company

EDIBLE FRENCH

ISBN 978-0-399-16984-7

First edition: October 2014

PRINTED IN THE UNITED STATES OF AMERICA

10 9 8 7 6 5 4 3 2 1

Text design by Tiffany Estreicher
Illustrations by Mélina Josserand

CONTENTS

INTRODUCTION

One fall evening six years ago, I was having dinner at a small Paris bistro with two dear friends of mine who were visiting from California. As we studied the menu, we noticed it was decorated with dozens of French expressions related to food, printed in different retro types.

Once our orders had been placed, we asked to keep a menu and spent a happy moment translating, explaining, and finding English equivalents for those idioms. The seed of an idea was planted, and two weeks later I started a series of posts on my food blog, *Chocolate & Zucchini*, to shed light on what I dubbed the "edible idioms" of the French language.

I've always loved the idiosyncrasies of languages and what they tell us about a culture, and it is certainly striking to see the French love of food and the importance meals have in daily life translate so richly in the fabric of the language. Matters of the table are considered with such care and attention that whenever the French mind searches for an expression to illustrate a situation, it is likely to come up with a food-related metaphor or simile, one that has to do with bread or cheese or wine.

Researching those expressions was as much a treat for me as for my readers; this series soon became one of my most popular, and I was often asked whether I had plans to publish them as a book.

The spark for that came four years later, when Mélina Josserand first contacted me. A French watercolor artist living in London, she was a fan of those posts and was volunteering to illustrate them.

I was instantly smitten with the playfulness of her work and her eye for color, and after collaborating on a few posts and hitting it off like we'd known each other all our lives, we decided to turn my words and her brushstrokes into the book you are now holding in your hands.

In it you'll find fifty of the most delicious expressions of the French language, some of them favorites from the blog series, some of them all new, with example sentences and Mélina's gorgeous illustrations. You'll also find cultural notes, fun quizzes, and a few very easy but very tasty recipes inspired by some of these idioms.

We hope you enjoy this colorful window onto the French language and that you'll "make your honey out of it."

To listen to the audio recordings of the expressions and example sentences and to see pictures of the recipes included in this book, please visit the Edible French mini-site at http://cnz.to/ediblefrench or use the QR code below.

Comme un tablier
à une Vache

Aller à quelqu'un comme un tablier à une vache

Fitting someone like an apron fits a cow

This idiom is used to say a piece of clothing is **unbecoming or ridiculous** on a person.

It is a self-deprecatingly funny phrase to use on yourself but becomes unkind if you're referring to others: It implies that the person has tried to dress with elegance but lacks the class or figure to pull it off.

This expression is chiefly applied to women. A more masculine, though seldom-used equivalent is *ça lui va comme des guêtres à un lapin.* (It suits him like gaiters on a rabbit.)

Example

J'ai commandé une robe sur Internet, mais elle me va comme un tablier à une vache.

I ordered a dress online, but it fits me like an apron fits a cow.

Avoir de la bouteille

Having some bottle

This expression points out the **value, experience, and wisdom** that a person gains with age (take that, ageism!).

The idiom was originally used in reference to wine and other spirits, indicating that they had spent a number of years inside a bottle, as opposed to the casks or barrels of their young days.

This wasn't always meant as a good thing, as wine can fade when aged for too long. But in the nineteenth century, when the idiom began to be used for people, it took on an altogether positive note.

Example

Il nous faut un commercial qui ait plus de bouteille.

We need a salesman with more bottle.

Avoir de la Bouteille

Avoir du Pain
sur la Planche

Avoir du pain sur la planche

Having bread on the board

If you **have a lot of work to do**, you might say you have bread on the board.

Until the early twentieth century, the expression had another meaning entirely. It meant that your future was well provided for: You had enough bread stocked up that you wouldn't go hungry.

But when people grew accustomed to eating fresh bread rather than keeping loaves, the image started to evoke the uncooked ones that the baker lines up on a board to rise. It then shifted to mean that there was still much baking to do before the bread was ready to sell.

Example

Il faut que je fasse toute la facturation du trimestre ; j'ai du pain sur la planche !

I have to do the invoicing for the whole quarter; I have bread on the board!

Avoir la pêche

Having the peach

Having the peach means **being in top form**, in high spirits, with a lot of energy. It is an informal expression that is used in casual conversation only.

This expression first appeared in the 1960s and may have evolved from the word *pêche* as slang for the face or head.

You may also encounter these related, but somewhat less refined, variations: *avoir la patate* (having the potato), *avoir la frite* (having the French fry), and *avoir la banane* (having the banana).

Example

Dis donc, tu as l'air d'avoir la pêche ce matin !

Wow, you seem to have the peach this morning!

Avoir la Pêche !

Coeur d'Artichaut

Avoir un cœur d'artichaut

Having the heart of an artichoke

This expression is used for a person who **falls in love easily** and frequently, possibly with several people at the same time—an inadvertent heartbreaker.

It finds its origin in a saying that was popular in the nineteenth century: *Cœur d'artichaut, une feuille pour tout le monde.* (Artichoke heart, a leaf for everyone.)

Because the center of the artichoke is called its heart, it is natural to link it to matters of love, and this idiom suggests that each of the many leaves represents a different romantic interest.

Example

Il devrait se méfier de cette fille ; c'est un vrai cœur d'artichaut.

He should beware of this girl; she's a real artichoke heart.

C'est la fin des haricots

It's the end of the beans

When it's *la fin des haricots*, it means it's all over: **All hope is gone**.

Beans are a cheap, filling, and plentiful food, and they are dried and put aside for times of scarcity. When all your food supplies have been used up, and you are eating the last of your beans, it means you are in a precarious position indeed.

This expression is often used with a measure of irony. The speaker is likely trying to make light of a dire situation, or to put a less serious one in perspective, or to exaggerate its seriousness for comic effect.

Example

Si on perd ce client, c'est la fin des haricots !

If we lose this client, it's the end of the beans!

La fin des Haricots

De la Tarte

Ce n'est pas de la tarte

It's no tart

This idiom is used to describe something that is **tricky**, difficult to do or to handle.

If you wanted to express the opposite, that something is very easy, you would use the sibling expression, *C'est du gâteau.* (It's cake.) Both bring to mind their near twins in English, "easy as pie" and "a piece of cake."

Why associate the idea of ease with baked goods? Tarts and cakes aren't necessarily the simplest things to make in the kitchen, but these idioms are referring to the *eating* of said baked goods, which usually takes little effort.

Example

J'essaie de décoller ce vieux papier peint, mais ce n'est pas de la tarte !

I'm trying to remove this old wallpaper, but it's no tart!

Apple Tarte Fine

Tarte fine aux pommes

A tarte fine is a thin tart with no raised borders, which means it does not require a tart pan. This easy, caramelized version may have your guests tomber dans les pommes *(see page 107) from sheer bliss.*

SERVES 6

3 tablespoons high-quality unsalted butter, melted

3 tablespoons sugar

1 sheet store-bought, all-butter puff pastry, 8 to 10 ounces (220 to 280 grams), thawed if frozen

All-purpose flour, for dusting

3 small apples, about 1 pound (450 grams), peeled, cored, and thinly sliced into circles

Preheat the oven to 350°F (175°C).

Line a baking sheet with parchment paper and brush the paper with half the melted butter to form a 10-inch (25-centimeter) disk shape. Sprinkle with half the sugar.

Unfold the puff pastry onto a lightly floured counter and cut out a 10-inch (25-centimeter) circle using an upturned cake pan or plate as a template. (If the puff pastry is not large enough, roll it out with a lightly floured rolling pin to reach the appropriate size.)

Transfer the pastry circle to the prepared sheet, placing it on top of the buttered and sugared area.

Arrange the apple slices in an overlapping pattern, starting from the outside and leaving a ½-inch (1.5-centimeter) border. Brush the border and the apples with the remaining butter.

Place in the oven and bake for 30 minutes, until the apple slices feel soft when pierced with the tip of a knife. Sprinkle with the remaining sugar, and place under the broiler for 2 minutes, watching closely, until the sugar is caramelized.

Let cool and serve, slightly warm or at room temperature.

Changer de crémerie

Changing creameries

Changer de crémerie means **taking your business elsewhere** when you're unhappy with the service you're getting.

This idiom appeared in the early nineteenth century, and the word *crémerie* is to be understood as the place where one buys cream, butter, and cheese. (The modern term is *fromagerie*, which illustrates the shift of focus these shops have undergone; the modern customer goes in for the cheese and buys cream and butter as an afterthought.) At the time the expression was formed, however, creameries often doubled up as simple working-class restaurants, and the word was used more broadly for any drinking or eating establishment.

Example

Tous ses clients ont fini par changer de crémerie.

All his customers eventually changed creameries.

Changer de Crémerie

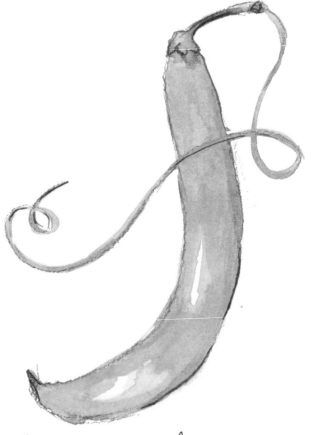

Courir sur le haricot

Courir sur le haricot de quelqu'un

Running on someone's bean

If someone says you're running on their bean, it means you are **getting on their nerves.**

This idiom appears to have merged from two similar expressions: *courir quelqu'un* (running someone) and *haricoter quelqu'un* (beaning someone), which both meant bothering someone. Because of the dried bean's shape, the word *haricot* has historically been slang for either the brain or the toe. In both cases, it's easy to imagine how exasperating it would be to have someone run around inside your head or across the tips of your feet.

Example

Elle commence à me courir sur le haricot à chanter sans arrêt !

She's starting to run on my bean with her incessant singing!

Écrire des tartines

Writing tartines

This expression means **being wordy**.

A tartine is a slice of bread topped with something that's easily spread, most typically butter, jam, or cheese. But in nineteenth-century journalists' slang, *une tartine* was a very long and very boring article or speech.

And because the baguette shape was introduced right around that time, I like to picture the writer or speaker fastidiously buttering a long piece of split baguette.

Example

Un paragraphe suffira ; ce n'est pas la peine d'en écrire des tartines.

One paragraph will do; no need to write tartines.

La Ville lumière a eu de multiple vies
voit encore les vestiges de la deuxième
lutèce la romaine, rue St Jacques
trace rectiligne de l'ancien Cardo
Maximus ou rue mouge, lorsque,
délice de printemps, on va s'asseoir
sur les gradins des arènes. Les trois
Capétiens ensuite entre le XI et le
siècle firent passer Paris du statut
petite cité à celui de Métropole, en
Notre-Dame et la Sainte Chapelle,
pavèrent les rues, édifièrent un
dont une portion se dresse encore rue

~ Écrire des Tartines ~

Tout un Fromage

En faire tout un fromage

Making a whole cheese out of it

If you **make a big fuss** about something and blow it out of proportion, you are making *tout un fromage* out of it.

This idiom is derived from the twentieth-century expression *en faire tout un plat* (making a whole dish out of it), which also evolved into *en faire tout un flan* (making a whole flan out of it).

The idea is that the person takes what little there is and turns it into something much more substantial. A few scraps into a whole dish; milk, eggs, and sugar into a whole flan; a little milk into a whole cheese.

Example

Il faut qu'on lui fasse valider ce courrier, sinon elle va en faire tout un fromage.

We have to run this letter by her, or she'll make a whole cheese out of it.

En rang d'oignon

In onion row

This expression means being lined up **in single file**.

The idiom most likely refers to the way onions are planted in a vegetable garden: carefully aligned in row upon row of raised beds.

A more colorful—but perhaps far-fetched—explanation summons the memory of Artus de la Fontaine-Solaro, Baron of Ognon. He was a master of ceremony in the sixteenth century, and as such, he was responsible for making sure guests were placed according to their rank (*rang* in French) in official celebrations.

Example

C'était adorable de voir tous les enfants en rang d'oignon sur la scène.

It was adorable to see all the kids in onion row on stage.

En rang d'Oignon

Entre la poire
et le Fromage

Entre la poire et le fromage

Between the pear and the cheese

This expression is used when something happens **unexpectedly during a casual moment**.

It refers to the end of a meal, when guests have had enough food and drink to feel utterly relaxed. They are reclining in their seats, conversation is flowing freely, and no one expects what happens then.

Perhaps you feel, as I long did, that the order of the terms sounds reversed: In modern France, you're more likely to eat cheese first, followed by a ripe pear. But this idiom dates back to a time when a sliced pear was served *before* the cheese course, to cleanse the palate.

Example

Entre la poire et le fromage, il a annoncé qu'il partait vivre en Australie.

Between the pear and the cheese, he announced he was moving to Australia.

Être comme un coq en pâte

Being like a rooster in dough

You are like a rooster in dough when you're feeling **cozy and pampered**, in a state of absolute contentment.

This expression illustrates an interesting trait of French popular wisdom, which considers it an enviable thing for an animal to finish its life in a delicious, luxurious dish: *coq en pâte* is an old French specialty in which a fatted chicken is stuffed, wrapped in a buttery short-crust blanket, baked until golden, and served with a port and truffle sauce.

Example

Quand il rentre chez ses parents, il est comme un coq en pâte.

When he goes home to his parents, he's like a rooster in dough.

Coq en Pâte

Être dans les choux

Être dans les choux

Being in the cabbages

Being in the cabbages means that you're **the very last one** in a competitive game or ranking.

This late-nineteenth-century expression was probably formed as a play on the similarity of sound between *échouer* (to fail) and *les choux* (cabbages).

The cabbage has long been a crucial part of the French peasant diet as an easy-to-grow, cheap, and plentiful vegetable, and this explains how frequently it shows up in idioms (see page 55).

Example

Ce n'est même pas la peine de compter les points ; je suis dans les choux !

No need to even keep score; I'm in the cabbages!

Être tout sucre tout miel

Being all sugar all honey

This idiom means **being ingratiating**, acting in an overtly affable, considerate, and polite way. It is used ironically, to point out that the person harbors negative feelings behind a cloying front.

The expression appeared in the seventeenth century and relies on the idea that sugar and honey are sweet indeed, but using too much is suspicious: What bitterness is the cook trying to hide underneath?

Example

Elle est tout sucre tout miel avec sa belle-mère, mais en réalité elle ne la supporte pas.

She's all sugar all honey with her mother-in-law, but in truth she can't stand her.

Tout Sucre
Tout Miel

Faire son Miel

Faire son miel de quelque chose

Making one's honey out of something

When you're **profiting from a situation**, you are said to make your honey out of it.

The image refers to bees, going from flower to flower to harvest nectar and pollen and turning it into honey. Although this process plays a crucial role in the plant's reproduction, in this idiom the bee is seen as taking advantage of the flower's resources.

Sixteenth-century philosopher Montaigne is credited with introducing the analogy. In his *Essays*, he writes that a child profits from the books he reads as a bee profits from the flowers it visits.

Example

Comme d'habitude, les journalistes ont fait leur miel des rivalités au sein du parti.

As usual, journalists have made their honey out of the rivalries within the party.

Radishes with Maître d' Butter

Radis au beurre maître d'hôtel

This delicious compound butter is traditionally used to top a grilled steak. But it does such wonders on fresh radishes, you will quickly find yourself with, quite literally, plus un radis (see page 62).

SERVES 6

½ cup (115 grams) high-quality unsalted butter, slightly
    softened
3 tablespoons (20 grams) finely chopped shallots
3 tablespoons (10 grams) finely chopped flat-leaf parsley
1 teaspoon freshly squeezed lemon juice
½ teaspoon fine sea salt
3 bunches of small pink or red radishes,
    about 10 radishes per guest, trimmed
Fresh baguette, for serving

Prepare the *maître d'hôtel* butter the day before.
In a medium bowl, put the butter, shallot, parsley,
lemon juice, and salt. Using a wooden spoon or spatula, incorporate all the flavorings into the butter.

Scrape the butter mixture out onto a sheet of parchment paper and roll into a log, about 1½ inches in thickness and 5
inches in length (4 by 12 centimeters). Tuck in the sides of the
parchment paper to wrap tightly, and place in the refrigerator
until ready to serve.

Divide the radishes among six plates, and place a ½-inch (1.5-centimeter) slice of the *maître d'hôtel* butter on each. To eat, top each radish with a small pat of the butter and eat with a bite of bread. Leftover butter can be wrapped in a freezer bag and frozen for up to a month.

Almond Honey with a Touch of Salt

Miel aux amandes avec une pointe de sel

Inspired by a pistachio honey from Sicily I once tasted, this is an irresistible spread. I like to make my honey out of it (see page 35) at breakfast, on a piece of sourdough toast.

MAKES A LITTLE OVER 1 CUP

⅔ cup (200 grams) raw honey
½ cup (120 grams) raw almond butter
1 teaspoon fine sea salt

In a bowl, put the honey, almond butter, and salt, and stir until thoroughly combined. Taste and adjust the seasoning.

Transfer to a jar, cover, and keep refrigerated until ready to use—spread thinly on toast or crêpes (see page 90), or scoop up with slices of tart apple.

Faute de grives,
on mange des merles

In want of thrushes, one eats blackbirds

This expression means that one must make do with what's available: **beggars can't be choosers**.

Thrushes and blackbirds are closely related game birds, but the former were traditionally held in higher regard by gastronomes, their flesh deemed more delicate.

All that's left of that custom is an idiom. French regulations now prohibit the sale of thrushes as an endangered species, so restaurants are no longer allowed to serve them, and neither bird is commonly consumed nowadays.

Example

Il s'est rabattu sur un hôtel médiocre, le seul qui avait encore des chambres ; faute de grives, on mange des merles.

He fell back on a mediocre hotel, the only one with any vacancy; in want of thrushes, one eats blackbirds.

Faute de
Grives ...
on mange

des Merles.

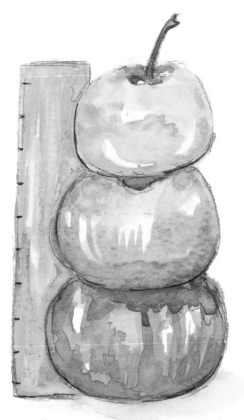

Haut comme
trois Pommes

Haut comme trois pommes

Three apples high

When someone, usually a child, is **small or very short**, he may be described as being *haut comme trois pommes*.

This idiom appeared in the early twentieth century, and I love how literal it is: Pile up three apples on the counter and you'll get an idea of just how short that person seems.

Peyo, the Belgian creator of the Smurfs—or rather *les Schtroumpfs*, as they are known in French—used this expression to describe their height, though clearly they'd have to be much smaller to fit inside the mushroom houses they inhabit.

Example

Comme tu as grandi ! La dernière fois que je t'ai vu, tu étais haut comme trois pommes !

How you've grown! The last time I saw you, you were three apples high!

La moutarde lui monte au nez

The mustard is rising to his nose

This expression means getting increasingly **impatient and angry**.

The French have a keen taste for mustard, and the jars sold in France are significantly sharper than the same brands manufactured for the American market—much to my dismay when I lived in the United States and started missing the kind I'd grown up eating.

So if you pop open a jar of real Dijon mustard, don't forget that it is at its most potent when freshly opened, or you'll feel its wrath course up the inside of your nose until your eyes water.

Example

Après plus d'une heure d'attente, la moutarde commençait à lui monter au nez.

After waiting for more than an hour, the mustard was beginning to rise to his nose.

La Moutarde

Le Gratin

Le gratin

The gratin

Gratin is the French term for casseroles baked in the oven until the surface becomes brown and crusty; it is also an expression that refers to a **social elite**.

It was originally a matter of class only, but now it extends to any milieu that values connections and popularity: *le gratin de la presse* for the most prestigious journalists, *le gratin parisien* for Parisian high society, *le gratin mondain* for socialites, and so on.

The expression is based on the idea that the browned top of the gratin is the part of the dish that's the most appreciated and sought after, just like the social elite.

Example

Le gratin du cinéma français assistera au cocktail.

The gratin of the French movie industry will attend the cocktail party.

Zucchini Gratin

Gratin de courgettes

*This is my mother's recipe for zucchini gratin, which she
would make throughout the summer when I was growing up.
And if I were to host* le gratin parisien *for dinner (see page 45),
it is one I would be proud to serve.*

SERVES 4 TO 6

2 teaspoons olive oil

2 pounds (900 grams) fresh zucchini (preferably small ones;
    they are sweeter and less watery), thinly sliced

2 teaspoons *herbes de Provence* (or a mix of finely chopped
    dried herbs such as thyme, rosemary, and oregano)

1 teaspoon fine sea salt

2 teaspoons couscous or fine-grind bulgur

3 large eggs

2 tablespoons crème fraîche or heavy cream

1 ounce (30 grams) freshly grated Comté cheese (substitute
    a good-quality Swiss cheese, if necessary)

Preheat the oven to 350°F (175°C).

Heat the olive oil in a large skillet. Add the zucchini, sprinkle
with the herbs and salt, and stir to combine. Cook over medium
heat until cooked through, 10 to 12 minutes, stirring regularly. If
the zucchini has rendered a lot of cooking juices, drain well.

Sprinkle the uncooked couscous on the bottom of a 10-inch

(25-centimeter) oval baking dish. Scoop up the zucchini with a slotted spoon and arrange it over the couscous.

In a medium bowl, whisk together the eggs and crème fraîche. Pour evenly over the zucchini, and top with the cheese.

Place in the oven and bake for 30 minutes, until set and golden brown. Let rest for 10 to 15 minutes before serving, as a side or as the main attraction.

Long comme un jour sans pain

Long like a day without bread

This expression is used to bemoan a thing or an event that is **very long and dreary**.

Like most French idioms having to do with bread, this one dates back to a time when bread was the main component of the common person's diet: If there was no bread to be had, it meant that there was, in fact, no food at all.

And if you were to fast for an entire day, surely that day would feel excruciatingly long.

Example

Le discours du maire était long comme un jour sans pain.

The mayor's speech was long like a day without bread.

Long comme un jour
sans Pain

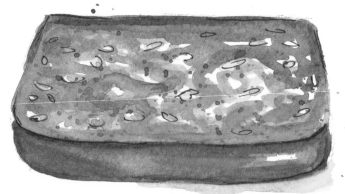

Manger son Pain Blanc

Manger son pain blanc

Eating one's white bread

Shortened from *manger son pain blanc le premier* (eating one's white bread first), this idiom means **starting with what's easiest** or most pleasant. It is used when a person has been enjoying a comfortable situation obliviously and is in for a rude awakening.

The expression appeared in the sixteenth century, when refined flour and white bread were a luxury and common people ate *pain noir* (black bread), made with roughly milled flours.

I find it a good way to determine a person's life philosophy: Given a loaf of good bread and one of an inferior sort, would you save the best for last or chose to eat your *pain blanc* first?

Example

Il a mangé son pain blanc, mais le plus dur reste à faire.

He has eaten his white bread, but the hardest is yet to come.

Ménager la chèvre
et le chou

Sparing the goat and the cabbage

If you are trying to **please both sides** in a situation in which the two parties are irreconcilable, you are sparing the goat and the cabbage.

The contention between goat and cabbage is clear. The goat wants to munch on the cabbage, but the cabbage would rather not, and the person responsible for them would have a hard time keeping both happy.

This thirteenth-century idiom is based on a version of the river-crossing riddle that involves a wolf, a goat, and a cabbage (see page 54).

Example

Il essaie de ménager la chèvre et le chou, mais au bout du compte personne n'est content.

He tries to spare the goat and the cabbage, but in the end nobody's happy.

Ménager la Chèvre
et le Chou

The Goat and the Cabbage

The riddle I mention on page 52 goes like this.

A man is standing on the bank of a river. He is traveling with a wolf, a goat, and a cabbage and needs to get them all on the other side. There is a small rowing boat he can use, but only one passenger can embark with him at a time (for the purpose of this riddle, the cabbage counts as a passenger).

The problem is this: If the man leaves the goat alone with the cabbage on the bank of the river, the goat will think it's lunch. Likewise, if the wolf and goat are left to their own devices, the wolf will devour the goat. On the other hand, the wolf doesn't enjoy cabbage all that much and can be trusted to leave it alone. So, what's the man to do in order to get everyone across safe and sound?

Here's the optimal solution: (1) the man gets the goat across and comes back empty, (2) he gets the cabbage across and brings back the goat, (3) he gets the wolf across and comes back empty, (4) he gets the goat across, and the four of them can go on their merry way.

Onions and Cabbages

Onions and cabbages, two staples of the French peasant diet, frequently appear in French idiomatic expressions.

In addition to *en rang d'oignons* (in onion row) on page 24, *être dans les choux* (being in the cabbages) on page 31, and *ménager la chèvre et le chou* (sparing the goat and the cabbage) on page 52, consider: *s'occuper de ses oignons* (minding one's onions) for minding one's own business, *aux petits oignons* (with small onions) for something that's been done with great care, *mon petit chou* (my little cabbage) as a term of endearment, *faire ses choux gras* (making one's greasy cabbages) for making a profit out of something lowly, *bête comme chou* (silly as cabbage) for something that's very simple, and *faire chou blanc* (making white cabbage) for coming up empty.

De l'eau dans son vin

Mettre de l'eau dans son vin

Putting water into one's wine

Putting water into your wine means **compromising**, deciding to adopt a more moderate stand on an issue or in an argument.

Pouring a little water in your wineglass was once accepted practice, when wine-making techniques were a bit hazy and cheap wines hard to swallow. Diluting the wine would then make it milder and easier to drink. Figuratively speaking, if you cut your views with a little water, you make them easier to agree to.

Example

Tu devrais mettre de l'eau dans ton vin, sinon tu ne vas jamais t'entendre avec lui.

You should put water into your wine, or you'll never get along with him.

Mettre du piment dans sa vie

Adding chili pepper to one's life

Heat lovers will agree that chili pepper makes any bland dish more interesting, and that is the premise of this idiom, which means **spicing up one's life**.

The expression also carries the idea that, whatever stimulating activity you've chosen to break out of your rut, it involves moderate risk taking and the thrill of doing something a little dangerous.

Example

Ils s'ennuyaient depuis le départ de leurs enfants, et cherchaient à mettre du piment dans leur vie.

They were bored since their children left home and were looking to add chili pepper to their life.

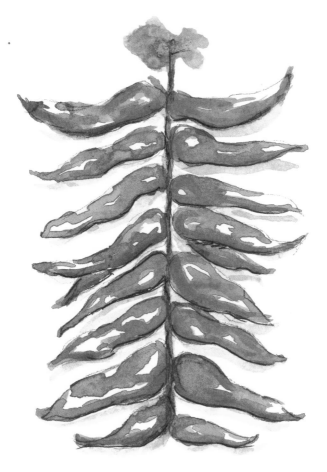

Mettre du Piment

Mettre son grain
de Sel.

Mettre son grain de sel

Putting in one's grain of salt

Mettre son grain de sel means **interfering** with a conversation or situation.

Originally, the grain of salt symbolized a witticism, a bon mot, thrown into a conversation to liven it up, as salt does a dish. But this expression now refers to any unsolicited comment or action.

I always imagine someone hovering near the stove and extending his arm, unprompted, to add a bit of salt to the dish as it is prepared. (And how maddening would that be?)

Example

C'est énervant, elle ne peut pas s'empêcher de mettre son grain de sel.

It's annoying how she can't help but put in her grain of salt.

N'avoir plus un radis

Not having a single radish left

This vegetable patch idiom means that you have **no money left**.

It is built on the word *radish* as slang for *un sou*, a penny in the old currency system that disappeared with *la livre* and *le denier* after the French Revolution, when *le franc* was first introduced.

Small fruits and vegetables are often used in the French language to illustrate things of little value—*des nèfles* (loquats, for trifles), *un navet* (a turnip, for a very bad show)—and the radish has probably come to mean a penny as a similar-sound derivation from the older slang *un rond* (a circle).

Example

Tu peux m'avancer vingt euros ? Je n'ai plus un radis.

Can you lend me twenty euros? I don't have a single radish left.

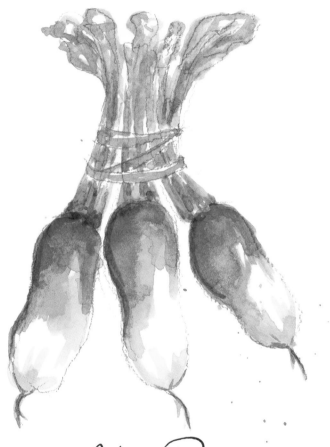

Un Radis

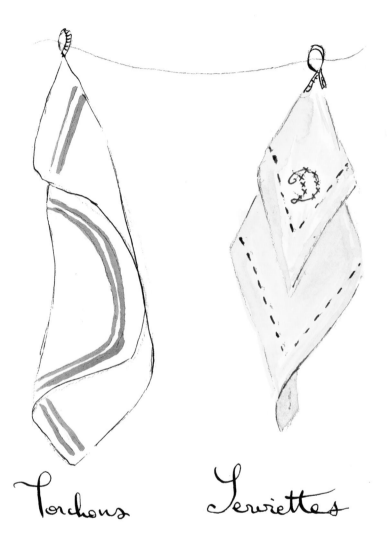

Torchons   Serviettes

Ne pas mélanger les torchons et les serviettes

Not mixing dishtowels with napkins

This expression means **treating things or people differently** according to their value or class.

It opposes the dishtowel, a lowly rag used for domestic chores, and the napkin, a distinguished piece of cloth that is part of an elegant table setting.

The classist implication was that the former belonged to the realm of servants, while the latter belonged to the world of their employers and their social life. It would then have been improper to wash or put them away together.

Example

On ne l'a pas mis à la table des mariés ; on ne mélange pas les torchons et les serviettes.

He wasn't seated at the bride and groom's table; you don't mix dishtowels with napkins.

Ne pas pouvoir être au four et au moulin

Not being able to be at the oven and at the mill

If you want to point out that you **can't do everything at once,** you might say that you can't be at the oven and at the mill.

This seventeenth-century expression stems from a time when each household milled its own grain and baked its own bread, using the communal mill and oven owned by the local lord. Naturally the baker had to execute these tasks in order, and it would have been impossible to do both at once.

Example

Il faut que j'embauche quelqu'un pour m'aider ; je ne peux pas être au four et au moulin.

I have to hire someone to help me; I can't be at the oven and at the mill.

Farine
Type 45

Au four et au Moulin

À quelle Sauce...?

Ne pas savoir à quelle sauce on va être mangé

Not knowing what sauce one is going to be eaten with

If your **fate is uncertain**, you may wonder what sauce you're going to be eaten with.

This eloquent idiom—I picture tiny humans wriggling in a soup plate as an ogre tries to decide between sauce Mornay and ketchup—is often used in situations describing opposing employees and employers or citizens and government.

The subject's fate is submitted to such a powerful force that he's beyond wondering whether he's going to be eaten; it's only a matter of finding out how exactly.

Example

L'usine vient d'être vendue, et les ouvriers ne savent pas à quelle sauce ils vont être mangés.

The factory was just sold, and the workers don't know what sauce they're going to be eaten with.

Papa gâteau

Cake daddy

A *papa gâteau* is a **doting father**, one who's affectionate and good-natured and allows his children to wrap him around their little finger.

A mid-nineteenth-century idiom, it derives from the verb *gâter*, which means spoiling or pampering a child. I am quite fond of it because my father was always the *papa gâteau* kind and also unapologetically sweet-toothed.

The expression can be applied to other members of a family—*maman gâteau* (doting mother), *tata gâteau* (doting aunt), *mamie gâteau* (doting grandmother), *tonton gâteau* (doting uncle)—but the father version is the one most often used.

Example

C'est un vrai papa gâteau avec sa dernière fille.

He's a real cake daddy with his youngest daughter.

Papa Gâteau

Pédaler dans
la Choucroute

Pédaler dans
la choucroute

Pedaling in sauerkraut

This idiom means **being in over one's head**, with the added notion that every effort made to get out of this mess is fruitless or makes things worse.

The image is clear enough: Picture yourself riding a bicycle on a big platter of Alsatian *choucroute*. Can you feel your wheels slipping against sausages and digging into steamed potatoes, as you gradually sink deeper and deeper in pickled cabbage?

You may come across the sibling expression *pédaler dans la semoule* (pedaling in couscous), an equally evocative variation.

Example

J'essaie de résoudre ce problème de maths, mais honnêtement, je pédale dans la choucroute.

I'm trying to solve this math problem, but frankly, I'm pedaling in sauerkraut.

Plein comme un œuf

Full as an egg

A thing or a place that's **completely full** is described as being *plein comme un œuf.* The reasoning is easy to understand: The white and yolk of an egg fill the shell entirely, and it would be impossible to squeeze anything more inside.

Nitpickers might argue that as it ages, an egg develops an air pocket inside, until it's not so full anymore. Perhaps a more accurate version of the expression might then be *plein comme un œuf fraîchement pondu* (full as a freshly laid egg).

Example

Je n'ai pas pu monter dans le métro ; il était plein comme un œuf.

I couldn't get on the metro; it was full as an egg.

Plein comme un Oeuf

Prendre de la Brioche

Prendre de la brioche

Gaining brioche

If you want to tell someone he's **growing a potbelly**, perhaps you can break it to him gently by using this endearing French idiom.

I once learned that the German word for a potbelly is *Bierbauch* (beer belly), but I will argue that the French idea of the brioche is even more expressive: It, too, points out a probable cause of the potbelly, but it does a better job of describing its shape and consistency.

Example

Quand il s'est rendu compte qu'il commençait à prendre de la brioche, il s'est inscrit dans un club de gym.

When he realized he was beginning to gain brioche, he signed up at a gym.

French–English Near Twins

The French and the English languages have a few of
these edible idioms in common. Can you guess the
English equivalents to the following?

La cerise sur le gâteau …

… the cherry on the cake.

Mettre tous ses œufs dans le même panier …

… putting all your eggs in one basket.

Séparer le bon grain de l'ivraie …

… separating the wheat from the chaff.

On ne peut pas faire une omelette sans casser des œufs …

… you can't make an omelet without breaking a few eggs.

Pousser comme un champignon …

… growing like a mushroom.

Cheveux poivre et sel …

… salt-and-pepper hair.

Marcher sur des œufs …

… walking on eggshells.

Se vendre comme des petits pains …

… selling like hotcakes.

C'est du gâteau …

… it's a piece of cake.

The French Do Like Their Bread

In my research I have found that bread is the most frequently used motif in food-related French expressions. This comes as no surprise when you consider the prominent role it has played in the humble man's diet for centuries.

We've examined *avoir du pain sur la planche* (having bread on the board) on page 5, *manger son pain blanc* (eating one's white bread) on page 51, *long comme un jour sans pain* (long like a day without bread) on page 48, and *prendre de la brioche* (gaining brioche) on page 77.

But I was also tempted to include *se vendre comme des petits pains* (selling like dinner rolls) for something that sells like hotcakes; *ça ne mange pas de pain* (it doesn't eat any bread) for something that doesn't cost much and is worth a try; *être bon comme le pain* (being as good as bread) for a good, amiable person; *pour une bouchée de pain* (for a bite of bread) for something sold at a very low price; *ôter le pain de la bouche de quelqu'un* (removing the bread from somebody's mouth) when you're robbing something from someone who's in dire need of it; and *ne pas manger de ce pain-là* (not eating that kind of bread) to express one's high moral standards.

Prendre le melon

Getting the melon

If people think you've become **too big for your britches**, they will say you've gotten the melon.

Melon is slang for head, because of the size and shape of the fruit, and this idiom is a variation on the expression *prendre la grosse tête* (getting the big head). It expresses that a person has let success go to his head so badly that his head is getting overblown. It is sometimes taken a step further to say *Il ne passe plus les portes* (He can no longer get through doorways), so big the head has become.

Example

Depuis que son film a été sélectionné pour le Festival de Cannes, il a vraiment pris le melon.

Ever since his film was selected for the Cannes Festival, he has really gotten the melon.

Prendre le Melon

Presser le Citron

Presser le citron à quelqu'un

Squeezing someone's lemon

We don't give a moment's thought about squeezing a lemon for juice then tossing its peel, but how does the lemon feel about it? Don't you think it feels a little used?

At least that is the premise of this idiom, which means **squeezing someone dry**—exploiting a person to get the maximum benefit out of the relationship.

Example

Si j'étais à sa place, je ne laisserais pas mon patron me presser le citron comme ça.

If I were in his shoes, I wouldn't let my boss squeeze my lemon like that.

Raconter des salades

Telling salads

This expression means **fibbing**, telling lies.

Originally, the expression meant telling a muddled or incoherent story. The idea was that a salad could be a jumble of ingredients all tossed together with no rhyme or reason. Not the kind of salad you or I make, of course, but I'm sure you've come across those too.

Over time, the expression gradually shifted to mean telling falsehoods. Indeed, in a salad bowl, wouldn't it be easy to hide a few lies in the midst of other truths?

Example

Je ne la crois plus ; elle m'a raconté tellement de salades!

I don't believe her anymore; she has told me so many salads!

Raconter des Salades

Comme un Soufflé

Retomber comme
un soufflé

Falling back like a soufflé

This idiom describes **a short-lived success**, an idea or a project that runs out of steam in a quick and sudden way.

If you've ever attempted to make a soufflé, you know what it's like: The egg white–raised preparation is indeed quick to deflate. And while the fresh-out-of-the-oven, puffy soufflé is sure to garner admiring gasps from the crowds, will its sunken version sustain their interest?

Example

Au début, les gens ne parlaient que de ça, et puis c'est retombé comme un soufflé.

Initially it was all people talked about, and then it fell back like a soufflé.

Retourner quelqu'un comme une crêpe

Flipping someone like a crêpe

This expression means **changing someone's mind very easily**.

It refers to the typical crêpe-making technique in which you flip the crêpe in the pan with a swift jolt of the wrist.

Crêpes are eaten in France to celebrate *la Chandeleur* (Candlemas) on February 2, a holiday that marks the Presentation of Jesus at the Temple. On that day, French superstition has you hold a coin in your left hand while you attempt to flip a crêpe with the right; if it falls back smoothly, your year will be one of happiness and prosperity.

Example

Il voulait faire du camping, mais je l'ai retourné comme une crêpe ; on ira à l'hôtel !

He wanted to go camping, but I flipped him like a crêpe; we'll stay at a hotel!

Comme une Crêpe

French Crêpes

Crêpes sucrées

Celebrate Candlemas or Mardi Gras with a fresh batch of French crêpes. And if anyone objects to it, a golden round dotted with butter and sprinkled with sugar should be enough to flip that naysayer comme une crêpe (see page 88).

MAKES ABOUT FIFTEEN 9½-INCH (24-CENTIMETER) CRÊPES

2 cups (250 grams) all-purpose flour
¼ cup (50 grams) sugar
¼ teaspoon fine sea salt
3 large eggs
1 cup (240 milliliters) milk
1 cup (240 milliliters) water
2 tablespoons rum (optional)
Vegetable oil for cooking

Combine the flour, sugar, and salt in a large mixing bowl, and form a well in the center. Crack in the eggs, one by one, stirring them in gently with a whisk to incorporate with some, but not all, of the dry ingredients.

Pour in the milk, then the water, slowly, whisking as you pour. Keep whisking until all the flour is incorporated; the batter will be thin. Add the rum, if using, and whisk again. Cover and refrigerate for at least 2 hours, and preferably overnight.

Remove the batter from the fridge and whisk it again. Set a

thick-bottomed, low-rimmed skillet over high heat. When it is hot, brush it lightly with oil.

Ladle just enough batter into the pan to cover it thinly, and swirl the pan around to form a round disk. Cook until the top is set and the edges start to pull away from the sides of the pan, about 1 minute. Run the tip of a hard spatula around the crêpe to loosen, peek underneath, and flip it when you see that it is nice and golden.

Cook the other side until golden, about 30 seconds, and slip it out of the pan onto a plate to serve. Grease the skillet again every two crêpes, or as needed.

Se faire rouler
dans la Farine

Se faire rouler dans la farine

Being rolled in flour

Being rolled in flour means **being fooled,** naively taken advantage of by someone who's wittier and smarter.

This expression dates back to the early nineteenth century. *Rouler quelqu'un* means cheating or swindling somebody, and the flour symbolizes lies, or misleading arguments, because things covered in flour can't be properly recognized.

It also adds a notion of ridicule: The victim is the only one who didn't see that sack of flour coming, and now he's covered in it for all to laugh at.

Example

Si tu es trop gentil avec elle, elle va te rouler dans la farine.

If you're too nice to her, she'll roll you in flour.

Se fermer comme une huître

Closing up like an oyster

If someone wants to talk to you about something and you refuse to speak, you might be described as closing up like an oyster—in short, **clamming up**.

It's no wonder both the English and the French use some of their favorite bivalve mollusks to express that idea: At the bottom of the sea, they keep their "mouths" wide open to catch food particles but shut them firmly as soon as danger looms—and good luck prying them open after that.

Example

J'ai essayé de lui parler, mais elle s'est fermée comme une huître.

I tried to talk to her, but she closed up like an oyster.

Une Huître

Serrés comme des Sardines

Serrés comme des sardines

Huddled together like sardines

This expression is used when a group of people is **squeezed into a very small space** with no room to move.

It refers to canned sardines, which are indeed packed into the can as tightly as they'll fit. The earliest version of the expression specified *serrés comme des sardines en boîte* (huddled together like canned sardines) but the last part was soon dropped.

Lesser-known variations on this expression are *serrés comme des harengs* (huddled together like herring) and *serrés comme des harengs en caque*, the *caque* being the barrel in which herring is layered for salt curing.

Example

On était serrés comme des sardines dans cette tente minuscule.

We were huddled together like sardines in this tiny tent.

Sardine Spread with Cumin and Dates

Tartinade de sardine au cumin et aux dattes

If you feel bad for canned sardines because they're serrées comme des sardines in their tin can (see page 97), this spread is a delicious way to set them free. It is wonderful as a sandwich filler, on crackers, or eaten with vegetable sticks.

MAKES 1¼ CUPS

2 (4-ounce; 115-gram) cans
   high-quality sardines
   packed in olive oil
¼ cup (60 milliliters) yogurt
1 small bunch fresh chives

2 Medjool dates, pitted
1 tablespoon freshly
   squeezed lemon juice
1 teaspoon ground cumin
¼ teaspoon fine sea salt

Drain the sardines from the cans, reserving the olive oil for another use. Put the sardines in the bowl of a food processor with the yogurt, chives, dates, lemon juice, cumin, and salt. Process until smooth. Taste and adjust the seasoning. Serve with crackers or vegetable sticks.

Flourless Lemon Soufflés

Soufflés au citron sans farine

Soufflés don't have to be a daunting affair, as these simple lemon ones attest. Yet their impression on your taste buds will be a long-lasting one that won't retomber comme un soufflé (see page 87).

SERVES 6

2 teaspoons unsalted butter

¼ cup (50 grams) sugar, divided

1 organic lemon

4 large eggs

3 tablespoons (20 grams) almond meal

¼ teaspoon salt

Preheat the oven to 350°F (175°C). Grease six 4-ounce (120-milliliter) ovenproof ramekins with the butter up to the rim. Sprinkle the bottom and sides with ½ teaspoon of the sugar each. Reserve in the refrigerator.

Finely grate the zest from the lemon, and squeeze the fruit to get 3 tablespoons juice. Set aside.

Separate the eggs, keeping all 4 egg whites but only 3 yolks.

In a medium bowl, whisk together the egg yolks, remaining sugar, almond meal, lemon zest, and lemon juice.

In a separate, thoroughly grease-free bowl, beat the egg whites with the salt until stiff. Fold delicately into the egg yolk mixture with a spatula.

Fill the ramekins at two-thirds capacity and bake for 10 to 12 minutes, until puffy and golden. Serve immediately.

Tarte à la crème

Cream pie

When someone utters **a banality**, a commonplace idea that is rehashed and used in place of a fresh, original thought, you may be tempted to roll your eyes and call it a *tarte à la crème*.

A simple tart shell garnished with pastry cream, this specialty from the north of France owes its idiom stardom to seventeenth-century playwright Molière. In his *Critique de l'École des Femmes*, he included a scene in which a character keeps chanting *"Tarte à la crème ! Tarte à la crème !"* instead of contributing to the debate.

Example

Dire que les enfants d'aujourd'hui sont moins bien élevés qu'avant, c'est vraiment une tarte à la crème.

Saying that today's children are not as well behaved as they used to be is really a cream pie.

Tarte à la Crème

La dragée haute !

Tenir la dragée haute

Holding the candied almond high

Dragées are a traditional French confection made of whole almonds covered with a smooth sugar coating that is tinted with various pastel colors. They are typically given out as party favors at weddings and christenings.

And *tenir la dragée haute* means **making someone beg and plead**; children and small dogs are particularly attracted to candy, and if you were to hold a *dragée* just high enough for it to be out of reach, they would be jumping and whimpering to get to it.

Example

Comme tout l'argent du couple est à elle, elle tient la dragée haute.

Since all the couple's money is hers, she holds the candied almond high.

Tomber comme un cheveu sur la soupe

Falling like a hair on soup

This early-twentieth-century idiom means **being inappropriate or incongruous**, out of place in an obnoxious way.

If you find the idea of a hair in your soup plate fairly unappetizing, you may be surprised to learn that in the context of this expression, it causes no particular disgust. It is merely seen as an annoyance, something that diverts the eater's attention from what's really important: the soup.

Example

A chaque fois qu'il ouvre la bouche en réunion, ses commentaires tombent comme un cheveu sur la soupe.

Every time he opens his mouth during meetings, his comments fall like a hair on soup.

Un cheveu sur
la Soupe

AMBROSETTE de NORMANDiE

10 kg

Tomber dans les Pommes

Tomber dans les pommes

Falling into the apples

This expression means **passing out**.

There is no definitive explanation of this idiom's origin, but it is most likely a distorted version of *tomber dans les pâmes*, related to *se pâmer*, an old-fashioned word for swooning or fainting.

I myself always vaguely thought that *tomber dans les pommes* meant that if you fainted near a pile of apples, you'd fall right into them, which I imagine you would.

Example

Dès que l'infirmière a sorti la seringue, il est tombé dans les pommes.

As soon as the nurse took out the needle, he fell into the apples.

Tourner au vinaigre

Turning to vinegar

A **situation or a conversation that's taking a bad turn** and may get ugly very soon is thought to be turning to vinegar.

The phrase originally refers to wine, when the action of bacteria makes it ferment and turn to vinegar or when the wine simply spoils and its flavor turns sour. (The word *vinaigre* comes from *vin aigre*, or sour wine.)

Because wine is considered nobler—and certainly nicer to drink—than vinegar, the image was gradually adopted to describe something good that morphs into something unpleasant.

Example

J'ai mis fin à la discussion avant qu'elle tourne au vinaigre.

I put an end to the discussion before it turned to vinegar.

Tourner au Vinaigre

Traîner des Casseroles

Traîner des casseroles

Dragging saucepans

We've evoked many kinds of ingredients so far, but they wouldn't be much without cooking utensils, so I couldn't pass up the opportunity to feature the most ubiquitous one: the saucepan. In the French language, the clang of dragging saucepans is the image used for someone who's **bearing the weight of a past mistake**, or just the suspicion of one.

And indeed, this kind of baggage is likely to follow a person around for years in an embarrassing and noisy way, like a saucepan tied to a dog's tail as a cruel prank.

Example

Comme tous les hommes politiques, il traîne quelques casseroles.

Like all politicians, he drags a few saucepans.

Vouloir le beurre et l'argent du beurre

Wanting the butter and the money for the butter

This idiom expresses an unreasonable or unrealistic **desire to have it both ways**.

It appeared in the twentieth century and refers to someone who's going out to buy butter and expects to come home with the butter and the same amount of money in his pocket.

A humorous variation goes, *vouloir le beurre, l'argent du beurre et le sourire de la crémière* (wanting the butter, the money for the butter, and the dairymaid's smile). More ribald variations feature other parts of the dairymaid's anatomy, but I will spare you those.

Example

Si tu ne veux pas qu'elle s'en mêle, il ne faut pas lui demander de t'aider : tu ne peux pas avoir le beurre et l'argent du beurre.

If you don't want her to meddle, you shouldn't ask for her help: You can't have the butter and the money for the butter.

Le Beurre et
l'argent du Beurre

Quiz Time!

Now that you've learned about this book's fifty expressions, try answering these questions.

What vegetable is the symbol of a French heartbreaker?

The artichoke—see page 9.

What garment is particularly ill-fitting on a French cow?

An apron—see page 1.

What condiment rises to their nose when the French get angry?

Mustard—see page 42.

What fruit do the French fall into when they faint?

Apples—see page 107.

What cookware are the French said to be dragging around when the past is haunting them?

Saucepans—see page 111.

What fruit do the French associate with being in high spirits?

The peach—see page 6.

What do the French add to their wine when making a compromise?

Water—see page 57.

In the French language, what vegetable is associated with being lined up neatly?

Onions—see page 24.

What fish lives in particularly close quarters?

Sardines—see page 97.

What French dessert is the symbol of a rehashed idea?

The cream pie—see page 100.

ACKNOWLEDGMENTS

From Clotilde: Let me start with a word of thanks to Shelli and Gene Oreck, who witnessed the birth of the Edible Idiom idea, and whose friendship and support have meant so much to me over the years.

Thank you also to Maxence, for adding food-related expressions to the Ever-Expanding List and for inventing silly ones to make me laugh (these are not featured in the book).

Endless thanks and a hug to Mélina Josserand, who is an absolute delight to work with, and whose illustrations I would like to eat for breakfast daily, so happy they make me.

Thank you to my wonderful editor, Meg Leder, and everyone at Perigee who helped bring this book to life with such passion and commitment: John Duff, Jennifer Eck, Tiffany Estreicher, Nellys Liang, Kellie Schirmer, and Melissa Broder.

I am just as thankful to Claudia Cross, my agent and friend of ten years, for seeing me through yet another project with talent and grace.

Finally, a special note of gratitude to my parents, Sylvie and Patrick, for passing on their love of dictionaries to me, for correcting my grammar as soon as I started talking, and for using English as their secret language, which made us girls want to learn it ever so badly.

From Mélina: Mille Mercis to Clotilde for her intuition and trust in me.

Loving thanks to my smiling husband, Emmanuel, for his time, support, and presence in all of our projects.

Thank you to my daughter Chloé for her keen artistic eye and delicious baking, and to Charlotte, Célestine, and Arthur for not crayoning all over the original illustrations.

And thank you to Maman and Papa for giving me love, and the love of art.

SOURCES

I referred to the following sources to write this book; my gratitude goes to their respective authors:

Centre National de Ressources Textuelles et Lexicales. Available at cnrtl.fr.

Duneton, Claude, and Sylvie Claval. *Le Bouquet des expressions imagées : Encyclopédie thématique des locutions figurées de la langue française.* Seuil: Paris, 1990.

Expressio. Available at expressio.fr.

Guillemard, Colette. *Secrets des expressions françaises.* Bartillat: Paris, 2007.

Rat, Maurice. *Dictionnaire des expressions et locutions traditionnelles.* Larousse: Paris, 2008.

Rey, Alain, and Sophie Chantreau. *Dictionnaire des expressions et locutions.* Le Robert: Paris, 2006.

Weil, Sylvie, and Louise Rameau. *Trésors des expressions françaises.* Belin: Paris, 2008.

INDEX

Page numbers in *italics* indicate recipes.